PHILOSOPHERS OF THE SPIRIT

SPINOZA

PHILOSOPHERS OF THE SPIRIT

SPINOZA

Edited by

Robert Van de Weyer

Hodder & Stoughton
LONDON   SYDNEY   AUCKLAND

Copyright © 1998 Robert Van de Weyer

First published in Great Britain 1998.

The right of Robert Van de Weyer to be identified as the Editor of this
Work has been asserted by him in accordance with the
Copyright, Designs and Patents Act 1988.

1 3 5 7 9 10 8 6 4 2

British Library Cataloguing in Publication Data:
A record for this book is available from the British Library.

ISBN 0 340 69465 3

Typeset in Monotype Columbus by
Strathmore Publishing Services, London N7.

Printed and bound in Great Britain by
Mackays of Chatham PLC, Chatham, Kent.

Hodder and Stoughton Ltd,
A division of Hodder Headline PLC,
338 Euston Road, London NW1 3BH

CONTENTS

The first task of philosophers is to ask questions – the questions which lurk in all our minds, but which, out of fear or confusion, we fail to articulate. Thus philosophers disturb us. The second task of philosophers is to try and answer the questions they have asked. But since their answers are inevitably only partial, philosophers both interest and infuriate us. Their third and most important task is to stimulate and inspire us to ask questions and seek answers for ourselves.

The human psyche or spirit has always been the main – although not the only – focus of philosophy. And inevitably when the psyche is explored, the gap between religion and philosophy rapidly narrows. Indeed for philosophers in the more distant past there was no gap at all, since philosophy was an aspect of theology and even mysticism. Although religious institutions are now quite weak, questions of spiritual philosophy are being asked more keenly and urgently than ever.

This series is an invitation to readers, with no philosophical training whatever, to grapple with the great philosophers of the spirit. Most philosophy nowadays is served in the form of brief summaries, written by commentators. Each of these books contains an introduction to the life and ideas of the philosopher in question. But thereafter the reader encounters the philosopher's original words – translated into modern English. Usually the words are easy to follow; sometimes they are more difficult. They are never dull, always challenging, and frequently entertaining.

INTRODUCTION

His Genius

Spinoza has the unique distinction of having been declared a heretic by both the Jewish synagogue and the Christian church. Like many others of his time, he concluded that the orthodox theism of both Judaism and Christianity was inherently contradictory and absurd. But, unlike his follow sceptics, he remained devoutly spiritual, and developed an alternative religious philosophy which was highly attractive and plausible. Thus he represented a far graver threat to the Jewish and Christian establishment than those who rejected religion in its entirety. It is probably true that Spinoza's religious views are today more widely held in western countries than orthodox theism; but few acknowledge the genius and influence of the gentle philosopher.

His fundamental quarrel with orthodox theism is that it presents God as external to, and thus separate from, his creation. This leads to two impossible problems. Firstly, if God is external, how can any of his creatures gain any knowledge of him? Orthodoxy's answer is that God chooses to reveal himself in

9

various ways: through the words of prophets, through miracles and other signs, through historical events, and, according to Christians, through the person of Jesus Christ. But Spinoza pointed out that human beings cannot know there are communications from God, unless God is already present within creation guiding their minds and hearts.

Secondly, if an external God could be known, would he not appear either as appallingly brutal, or as utterly callous? Orthodox theism normally presents God as having laid down certain laws and rules for human beings; and as having instituted rewards for compliance and punishments for disobedience. Assuming they were aware of this divine system of justice, the only reason why people would break a divine law would be weakness – and weakness should not be a cause for punishment. Orthodox theism could escape this dilemma, Spinoza recognised, by portraying God as indifferent to human behaviour; but this would condemn humanity to moral anarchy, and also make religious faith redundant.

In delineating these dilemmas Spinoza was doing nothing new; indeed, they have troubled both Christian and Jewish writers since the earliest centuries. But whereas orthodox theologians have tried vainly to find answers, Spinoza altered the assumption on which the questions themselves are based. He did not deny the possibility that God is external to the universe; but the core of Spinoza's philosophy is that God is also internal – that he exists with the universe and permeates it.

Spinoza offers various logical arguments for the existence of God within the universe. But the real proof in Spinoza's view is direct perception: that if people look at the world around them with an open mind, they perceive its fundamental unity – that every object has a common substance. And its common substance is what we call God.

From this premise Spinoza creates a religious system which is quite different from Christian and Jewish orthodoxy. The common divine substance, according to Spinoza, is thought: through thought God creates and sustains the universe, and all the objects in it. Thus the divine attribute in human beings – and probably in other living creatures also – is the capacity for thought. When we perceive God in the world, and contemplate his presence, we are in effect aligning our own minds with his. This is not to say that a single human mind can comprehend the mind of God; rather each human mind is a tiny part of the divine mind, which is infinite.

If God is universally present, we cannot speak of particular objects or actions as good and bad, in the traditional sense; there are no objective rules or standards by which moral judgements can be made. On the contrary, what we call the laws of nature are really the divine laws; so morality really consists in living in harmony with nature. But since our knowledge of nature is necessarily limited, how can we alter this harmony? Spinoza offers the most ingenious – and, once recognised, rather obvious – solution. He suggests that, whatever theistic justifications pious people may offer, the real objective of all human choices and decisions is to maximise pleasure and minimise pain. Far from regretting this, Spinoza praises it, saying that our sense of pleasure and pain is the law of nature working within us; so, if we truly attain personal happiness, we shall thereby be living in harmony with nature.

The problem, according to Spinoza, is to determine the constituent elements of pleasure and pain. He observes that people frequently make two errors. Firstly, they interpret pleasure and pain solely in terms of their physical appetites, whereas in fact our emotions are far more important. Secondly, even when they recognise the importance of emotions, they allow themselves to be slaves to their immediate passions. Spinoza believes that people should look within themselves, and learn about the whole range of feelings, passions, appetites and emotions that can cause pleasure and pain. Then they should work out how each one can be properly fulfilled, in such a way that there is no conflict between them.

In terms of religious observance, Spinoza's system

had a stark implication, which was not lost on his opponents: prayer, in the sense of asking God for things, is utterly useless. Orthodox theism, in which God is outside nature, allows God to intervene in the natural cause of events, in response to human pleading. To Spinoza this notion merely highlights the absurdity of theism. If God permeates nature, and the laws of nature are his laws, then he cannot suspend the natural course of events for the convenience of particular individuals. But this does not mean that religion as a whole should be abandoned. On the contrary, Spinoza saw great value in a regular discipline of meditation, in which people reflect on God both around them and within them, and hence bring minds and emotions into unity with him.

Having grown up within a strictly orthodox environment, Spinoza never entirely shook himself loose from the tenets of theism. And the grip of theism led him into the muddle about human freedom which also confounds orthodox theology. Like his orthodox counterparts Spinoza continues to correct the omnipotence of God; and this implies that all events are determined by him. Yet religion and morality make no sense unless human beings can make free choices; and humans manifestly experience themselves as free. In fact the notion of divine omnipotence presumes that God is external to the universe. If God is within nature, and if human thought is an aspect of divine thought, then human freedom is an expression of God's freedom.

Spinoza is sometimes described as a transitional figure: he is simultaneously the last of the great religious philosophers, and also a prophet of the secular enlightenment. More accurately and pertinently, he is a devoutly spiritual human being, who developed a religious system which is plausible in an age of science, and also profoundly attractive and satisfying.

His Life

Benedict Spinoza was born in Amsterdam in 1632. The different forms of his first name, which in English means 'blessed', indicate the varied influences of his upbringing. At home he was called 'Bento', the Portuguese form. His family belonged to a substantial body of Jews which a few decades earlier had fled from Portugal to Holland to escape religious persecution. Spinoza's father Michael, who had probably arrived in Amsterdam as a child, became a rich and successful merchant, and also a leading figure in the Jewish synagogue in the city. Within the synagogue the young Spinoza was called 'Baruch', the Hebrew form; and it seems probable that Michael, impressed by his son's intelligence, wanted his son to become a rabbi. To this end he sent his son to the small college which the Jewish community had just established, to study Hebrew language, literature and theology.

By the age of 20 Spinoza was becoming dissatisfied with the narrow range of the college's curriculum; and was also beginning to doubt his Jewish faith. He decided to take lessons from a secular tutor, who taught him Latin to enable him to read the great works of classical and medieval philosophy. Spinoza soon concluded that he must abandon orthodox Judaism, and dedicate himself to the free and unconstrained pursuit of truth. He thus gave up his rabbinical training, and announced himself to be a philosopher. As a sign of the change he adopted the Latin form of his name, Benedictus.

Two years later his father died. His stepsister, the only other surviving offspring, claimed that by denying his Jewish faith Spinoza had forfeited his right to inherit his father's wealth; and therefore she should receive it instead. Spinoza contested this in court, and won. But immediately he handed the entire amount back to her, declaring that a philosopher should not be encumbered by worldly concerns. He was now forced to fend for himself. Paradoxically his rabbinical training saved him. The Jewish college insisted that all putative rabbis should acquire a manual skill, partly to prevent them becoming a burden to their congregations, and partly as an antidote to pride. Spinoza had learnt to grind glass for spectacle lenses; and from this time onwards he survived by plying this trade.

The leaders of the Jewish synagogues were anxious not to offend their Christian counterparts, who had warmly welcomed them to Holland; and they were also eager to maintain the unity and cohesion of their own community. Spinoza seemed to jeopardise both objectives. By now he was openly declaring that the Bible possesses no greater authority or wisdom than the works of Pluto and Aristotle, he was expressing doubts about the immortality of the individual soul, and he was accusing both Jewish and Christian theologians of portraying God in their own image. Several Jewish leaders had private meetings with Spinoza, begging him to keep silent. While he was sympathetic to their predicament, Spinoza replied that his commitment to the pursuit of truth must override all other considerations. So in July 1656 the synagogue formally excommunicated him, a move intended to absolve the Jewish authorities from all responsibility for his views. Spinoza was shocked at the severity of this sentence, and upset at being cut off from his community; and a few weeks later he wrote at length to the synagogue, trying to show that his views were compatible with orthodoxy. But he received no response.

The Christian clergy in Amsterdam had no hesitation in supporting the synagogue's condemnation of Spinoza's views; and they joined the Jewish leaders in pressing the civil authorities to ban Spinoza from the city. Spinoza seems to have left before a formal order was issued, and went to live for a short time in a nearby village. Although he appreciated the opportunity to think in peace, he was beset by a sense of spiritual loneliness. So in 1660 he moved to Rijnsburg near Leyden, to attach himself to a small Christian sect called the Collegiants. While remaining devoutly religious, and adhering to the highest moral standards, the Collegiants rejected all formal doctrine and had no clergy; instead they formed small groups, or 'colleges', in which they helped one another to discern the truth within their own souls.

During his stay with the Collegiants Spinoza began to express his ideas on paper. His first treatise, *On the Improvement of Well-Being*, opens with his famous declaration of intent. He states that experience has taught him the futility of all normal aims and ambitions, and the emptiness of conventional morality. So he commits his life to investigating whether there is some form of intrinsic goodness. He then analyses why the aims which most people pursue – which he summarises as wealth, fame and pleasure – cannot bring lasting happiness, but in fact propel people into a kind of living death. And he describes his own struggle to abandon these aims, adopting instead the material simplicity and obscurity which, in his view, a philosopher requires. He followed this with his second treatise, *God, Humans and their Well-Being,* in which he gives an outline of the ethical and theological system he is developing.

These two works impressed many of his contemporaries for their combination of mystical insight and philosophical rigour; and they infuriated others – both clergy and philosophers – for the same reason. Spinoza thus acquired the fame which he had deliberately tried to avoid. He took no pleasure in it, but took eager advantage of one of its consequences: other philosophers and theologians started writing to him, to seek his opinion on various matters, and he entered into sustained correspondence with many of them. His surviving letters from this period onwards often express his insights with a simplicity which his formal works mostly lack. One of his admirers, a wealthy aristocrat, offered Spinoza a substantial annual income, plus the promise to make him his sole heir. Spinoza refused, for the same reasons that he had earlier given up his own fortune.

In 1663 Spinoza moved to Voorburg, a village near the Hague, later moving into the Hague itself. He had already started writing his greatest work, *Ethics*, and by late 1665 it was virtually complete. In it he propounds a complete metaphysical, ethical and psychological system, laid out to strict rules of logic, with axioms, propositions, demonstrations, and corollaries. Subsequent commentators have observed non-requitals, and have cast doubt on some of the axioms on which the system rests. And the prose is often so complex, and so impersonal, that it is extremely difficult to read. But it contains numerous nuggets of profound wisdom and insight; and taken as a whole it presents a view of the universe and of the human soul which is at once coherent and mystical. It seems to use logic to carry the mind beyond the sphere of logic.

The pain of separation from his Jewish roots still nagged at Spinoza; and he feared that publication of *Ethics* would cause even greater offence to his erstwhile friends than his earlier writings. He also convinced himself that he might want to make revisions to it later. So he put the manuscript aside; and from time to time, right up to his death, he returned to it and tinkered with certain phrases. In the meantime he found himself sucked into the political fray. Soon after moving to Vourburg he had made friends with a senior politician, Jan de Witt, who was an ardent defender of the principles of free speech and tolerance on which the Dutch Republic had been founded. But in the 1660s these principles came under growing threat, especially from leading members of the Reformed Church, who wanted a more authoritarian style of government, imposing Christian standards on the people. Spinoza responded by writing a treatise which argued, on moral and theological grounds, the case for free opinion and free worship.

He published his treatise, which he entitled *Tractatus Theologico-Politicus*, in 1670. Despite his admiration for Jan de Witt, he lacked the courage to align himself publicly with him, so he kept the authorship anonymous. Despite this, the treatise aroused great interest, quickly running through five editions. It helped to polarise the political debate, with some treating it as a manifesto of freedom, while others, in the words of one critic, denounced it as an instrument 'forged in hell by a renegade Jew and the devil' – suggesting that Spinoza's attempt to conceal his identity had failed. Two years later Spinoza was strongly tempted to make a public protest when Jan de Witt was assassinated by his political enemies; but Spinoza's friends restrained him, fearing that he too would be killed.

Spinoza's reputation suffered a severe blow in 1675 when the French army, which was at that time occupying Utrecht, invited him to come and hear their terms for peace. The French calculated that Spinoza's reputation for integrity would mean that the Dutch people would listen to him. Spinoza fool-ishly accepted the French invitation, and spent several weeks at their military headquarters negotiating with their generals. But when he returned to the Hague, far from studying his proposals, the Dutch people accused him of treachery. Cursing his own naïvety, he turned away from politics and returned to his philosophical reflections. He prepared *Ethics* for the printers, but decided that it should not be published until after his death. He also continued to correspond with other thinkers, and became friends with the philosopher Leibniz.

He never ceased to earn his living through grinding optical lenses. But through constantly inhaling glass dust he contracted pulmonary disease. He died in 1677, aged only 45. Following his instructions he was buried in a church, according to the Christian rite.

His Writings

It is impossible to pick up any of Spinoza's works, and read it straight through from beginning to end. The logic is so dense and convoluted, and his terminology so eccentric, that even the most devoted admirer wearies after a few pages. For this reason he has never been widely read. Yet those over the centuries who have persevered have acknowledged him as one of the greatest philosophical and religious thinkers the western world has produced.

Commentators today mostly agree that the weakest aspect of Spinoza's work is that on which he prided himself most: his logic. The strongest feature is one that he barely recognised in himself: his spiritual insight. So in this book his two major philosophical works are distilled into a series of 'sayings' –

much in the way that the ideas of most great mystical and religious teachers are commonly presented. Much the same treatment is given to his letters, although the looser style allows for some longer extracts. Only his first published work, in which he declares his intentions as a philosopher, is given in the form of continuous paragraphs.

I
THE IMPROVEMENT OF WELL-BEING

Experience has taught me that all the normal aims and ambitions which people pursue are vain and futile. And I have learnt that the various objects of my fears are in themselves neither good nor bad, except insofar as my mind is affected by them. So I have finally decided to investigate whether there is some form of intrinsic goodness, which can be known by the human mind – whether, in fact there is something to discover and attain which would give me continuous, serene and unending happiness.

I say 'I have finally decided' because at first sight it seemed foolish deliberately to abandon what was certain, for the sake of something uncertain. I could see the benefits of fame and wealth, and that I would have to give up the pursuit of these objects, if I were seriously to devote myself to the search for something new and different. I recognised that if happiness is in fact achieved through fame and wealth, I would inevitably miss it. But equally I recognised that if happiness does not depend on fame and riches, and if I devoted myself to acquiring them, I would also fail.

So I debated whether it would be possible to arrive at this new principle, or at any rate become certain of its existence, without altering my existing way of life. To this end I tried hard to maintain my way of life, but my efforts proved futile. The ordinary surroundings of life, which (as their actions testify) most people value highly, may be classed under three headings: wealth, fame and pleasure. These things absorb the mind to such a degree that it is impossible to think about anything new and different.

Pleasure enthrals the mind, driving out any other considerations, as if pleasure was itself the serene good. But when pleasure is gratified, the heart sinks into melancholy, so that the mind is upset and unable to think clearly.

The pursuit of fame and riches is likewise absorbing, especially if such objects are sought simply for their own sake, in the belief that they constitute the highest good. Striving for fame is especially absorbing, because fame is always desired for its own sake, and becomes the ultimate purpose to which all actions are directed. Moreover, the attainment of wealth and fame, unlike pleasure, is not followed by melancholy and remorse. On the contrary, the more we acquire, the more we want, and so we strive even harder for them. Yet if our efforts are frustrated we are plunged into the deepest sadness. Fame has the further drawback that it compels those pursuing it to order their lives according to the opinions of others, despising what others despise, and valuing what others value.

So I saw that these ordinary objects of desire would be obstacles in the search for something different and new. Indeed I could see that they were opposed to that search. So I was forced to decide whether to abandon them; or whether to retain them on the grounds that it would be foolish to exchange things that were certain for something uncertain ... Intense reflection convinced me that, if my search for a new principle of happiness were successful, I would be abandoning certain evils for a certain good. I thus perceived that I was in a state of great danger, and I was urgently in need of some remedy. I was like a sick man who sees that he will soon be dead unless some medicine to cure his disease is quickly taken; and so with all his strength he looks for that medicine, vesting all his hope in finding it. The pursuit of wealth, fame and pleasure would lead me to a kind of living death; if I attained those objects, I would not possess them, but be possessed by them ...

The sickness arises from making external things the objects of our love; and so our happiness or unhappiness becomes wholly dependent on the quality of those objects. When something is not loved no quarrels will arise concerning it; no sadness will arise if it perishes; no envy will arise if another person possesses it; no fear will arise from the prospect of losing it; no hatred will arise from people competing for it. In short, something which is not loved cannot disturb the mind. All mental disturbance arises from loving something which is transient.

Yet to love something eternal and infinite feeds the mind with unadulterated joy; such joy is not mixed with any sadness. So that which is eternal and infinite is wholly to be desired, and to be strived for with all our strength.

When this truth came clear to my mind, I could not immediately and completely lay aside all love of wealth, fame and pleasure. Nonetheless, when my mind was engaged with these philosophical thoughts, I found the love of these former objects of desire grew weaker, and the urge to find a new principle of happiness grew stronger. This gave me great comfort, because I could see that the sickness from which I suffered was not so strong as to resist all remedies. At first the periods of relief were quite short. But gradually, as the principle of true goodness grew more clear in my mind, the periods became more frequent and longer.

It then occurred to me that the acquisition of wealth, pleasure and fame is only a hindrance if they are sought for their own sake, as ends in themselves. But if they are sought as means to a higher end, then they will not cause damage. Indeed, in certain circumstances they could even be helpful.

Let me state briefly what I mean by true goodness, and also the nature of the highest good. In the laws of nature we can perceive the eternal order. Yet in our weakness we are unable to live according to this order. So we yearn to alter our character in such a way that we are in harmony with the eternal order; and we devote ourselves entirely to this purpose. The highest good, therefore, is the acquisition of such a character. In other words, the highest good is perfect harmony between the human mind and the whole of nature.

This, then, is the end for which I strive. I want to change my character in this way, and I want others to join me in this endeavour. In fact, it is part of my happiness to lend a helping hand to others, so that others can see things as I do, and desire what I desire. In order to do this, I must understand as much of nature as is necessary in order to harmonise my mind with it; and I must form a social order which is most conducive to changing the human character on these lines.

2

GOD AND HAPPINESS

from *God, Humans and their Well-Being*

God is that being whose attributes are infinitely perfect in every way.

Nature consists of attributes which are infinitely perfect in every way. Thus the definition of Nature is the same as the definition of God.

God has everything in his understanding; and, owing to his infinite perfection, can know nothing more. Thus he has created everything in his understanding and has made everything so that it exists in Nature.

We see unity everywhere in Nature. If there were different substances in Nature, it would be impossible for them to unite with one another.

In Nature there can be no division of substance, but only in the mode of substance. If I want to divide water, I only divide the mode of substance, not the substance itself.

When we say that an individual has died or has been annihilated, this statement can only apply to a particular mode of humanity – that is to say, a particular bodily human being. It cannot apply to the substance on which humans depend for their existence.

Outside God there is nothing at all.

There can be only one being which exists through itself. All other beings are attributes of it.

God, with reference to his creatures and his works, is the cause; God is also the whole.

Since nothing can exist, or be understood, apart from an outside God, it follows that God is a cause of all things.

God is the productive cause of all his works; all activities ultimately come from God.

God is the immanent, not the remote, cause of everything, since all that he produces is within himself, and not outside him.

God is the principal cause of his works ... but not the provoking cause.

Things conceived by God cannot be conceived more perfectly than he conceives them, so all things made by God are so perfect that they come from him in perfect condition.

Since God is perfect, he could not have omitted to do what he has done. Since everything that God does is perfect, it would be an imperfection for him to have omitted anything that he has done.

Since all that happens is caused by God, all must be predetermined by him. Otherwise he would be mutable, which would be a great imperfection.

Predetermination of events by God must have been from eternity. Yet in eternity there is neither before nor after. Thus God could never have predetermined things in any other way than that which they are predetermined now – and have been from all eternity.

God desires the welfare and protection of all. If God were to desire that a certain venture did not exist, this would imply that the welfare and protection of this creature consisted in its non-existence – which would be self-contradictory. That is why we deny that God can omit anything that he does.

To say that God cannot omit anything that he does sounds to some people like blasphemy, because it seems to belittle God. But this comes from a misapprehension of what constitutes true freedom. To think that freedom is the ability to do or to omit something good or evil, is quite wrong. True freedom is being the first cause of something, and hence being in no way constrained or coerced.

God is the first cause, because there is no external cause outside him to coerce or constrain him.

There is a general and a special providence. The general providence is the divine presence in Nature by which all things are produced and sustained as parts of the whole. The special providence is the divine presence in each individual thing by which it strives to preserve its existence within the whole.

The capacity to think and understand is a direct creation of God. It is the true Son of God, created by him from all eternity, and immutable for all eternity. It has one function: to understand clearly and distinctly all things at all times. This understanding produces perfect and infinite satisfaction.

The terms 'good' and 'evil' describe relationships between things, not the things in themselves. We never say something is good except with reference to something which is not so good. So when we say something is good, we merely mean that it conforms to our idea of goodness.

There exist in Nature only things and actions. Good and evil are neither things nor actions. Therefore good and evil do not exist in Nature.

The thought of an individual person is an attribute of the thought of God. The form and motion of an individual person are attributes of the form and motion of God.

Without God no thing can exist and no thing can be understood. Thus God must first exist and be understood before particular things can exist and be understood.

Reason in itself has no power to lead us to happiness and well-being. Therefore we must ask whether another kind of knowledge has the power.

There is a kind of knowledge that does not derive from anything else, but is a direct revelation of the object to the mind. If that object reveals itself as beautiful and good, the soul necessarily is united with it. The body reveals itself as beautiful and good, and so the soul is united with the body. The same occurs with other objects. This is the kind of knowledge which evokes love.

We know God as a direct revelation of himself to the mind. And we apprehend him as supremely beautiful and good. Thus we must necessarily become united with him; and in this unity our happiness and well-being consists

We do not – indeed, we cannot – know God just as he is. It is sufficient to know him to some degree in order to be united with him. The same applies to the body. I cannot know my body just as it is; yet my soul is perfectly united with my body – and what exists between soul and body!

This knowledge of God is direct and immediate, because he is the cause of it.

We are so united with God by nature, that without him we can neither exist nor be known. Since there is such a close union between God and us, it is evident that we cannot know him except directly.

As a thing is more or less perfect, so the union of that thing with God is more or less perfect. As the whole of Nature consists in a single substance, all things are united through Nature – and hence are united with God.

The spiritual or substantial unity of Nature may be seen in relation to our own bodies. Through awareness of the body, and through feelings within the body, we come to know directly the spirit of life itself. And we find ourselves wanting to embrace that spirit of life, which is not itself corporeal, but which holds the parts of the body in unity.

As we grow in knowledge of the spirit of life, we are born again. The first birth took place when the soul became united with the body, bringing it to life. The second birth takes place when we become aware of that unity.

3
FIRST DIALOGUE ON GOD AS THE INNER CAUSE

———————◆———————

from *God, Humans and their Well-Being*

LOVE: I see, Understanding, that both my essence and my perfection depend on your perfection. And your perfection depends on the perfection of the object which you have conceived. So tell me: have you conceived one entity which is supremely perfect, and cannot be limited by any other entity; and am I part of that entity?

UNDERSTANDING: I consider that only Nature, in its infinite totality, is supremely perfect. But if you have any further queries, I suggest you ask Reason; she will clarify matters.

REASON: To me the truth of the matter is beyond doubt. If we were to try to limit Nature, we should have nothing with which to limit it, since Nature includes everything; and this would be absurd. We avoid this absurdity by stating that Nature is an eternal unity, infinite, omnipotent, and so on; that is, that Nature contains all that exists. The negative of Nature is thus nothing.

DESIRE: How wonderful it is to suppose that this unity in Nature is compatible with the difference and variations which I observe everywhere in Nature. But how can this be? I see that thought has nothing in common with material existence, and that one does not limit the other. If, in addition to these two entities, you wish to posit a third one which is perfect in all respects, then you are caught in manifest contradictions. You may try to separate this third entity from the other two; but then it will lack all the attributes of the other two, so cannot be perfect. Moreover, if this entity were omnipotent and perfect, it could only have attained perfection by having created itself; if another entity had created it, then this other entity would possess greater potency and perfection. Finally, if you call this third entity omniscient, then it must necessarily know itself; yet knowledge of oneself alone is inferior to knowledge of oneself together with knowledge of other entities. All these are manifest contradictions. So I would advise love to rest content with what I show her and not inquire about these deeper matters.

LOVE: You are utterly dishonourable. If I were to rest content with whatever you show me, I would be ruined by trusting myself to you, I would from that moment be persecuted by the two arch enemies of the human race – Hatred and Remorse, and sometimes also by Oblivion. So I turn again to Reason, and in doing so I silence these foes.

REASON: When you say, Desire, that there are different entities, you are wrong. I see clearly that there is only one entity, which exists through itself, and includes all things. You try to divide the mental and the material aspects, suggesting that they are entirely separate entities. But these are not separate in this sense; they are both dependent on the single entity, which we call Nature. The proof of this is that neither could exist on its own; it is impossible to conceive mental activity without a material context; and if there were a material entity entirely separate from mental activity, it would by definition be beyond the powers of conception. You would, I am sure, recognise that willing, feeling, understanding, loving and so on are all mental activities; they are different aspects of thought, and are part of a single entity. It follows from this that thought and matter can also be part of a single entity. They are only aspects of the one eternal, infinite being, who exists entirely in and through himself. Thus we can say for certain that there is unity; and nothing can be imagined outside this unity.

DESIRE: I think there is great confusion in your argument. It seems to me that you separate the whole from its parts – which is truly absurd. All philosophers are unanimous in saying that 'whole' is something that exists within the mind; and that there is nothing in Nature apart from human thought. Moreover, you seem to confuse whole with cause. As I have said, the whole only exists through its parts; yet you represent thought as including understanding, love, and so on. But you cannot call thought the whole; it is only the cause of these other things.

REASON: I see that you are mustering all your friends against me; and that, using the method generally adopted by those who oppose the truth, you are trying to achieve by quibbling what you cannot accomplish by your fallacious arguments. But you will not succeed in winning love to your side by such means. Your assertion is that the cause of all that exists – the originator of all effects – must be outside all that exists. But you say this because you can perceive only the immediate cause, not the inner cause. The inner cause cannot produce anything outside itself. This is exemplified by understanding, which both includes ideas and causes ideas. Insofar as ideas depend on understanding, then understanding is this cause; but since understanding consists of ideas, then understanding is the whole. In the same way, God is the cause – the inner cause – of all that exists; and he is also the whole.

4
SECOND DIALOGUE ON GOD AS THE INNER CAUSE

from *God, Humans and their Well-Being*

ERASMUS: I have heard you say, Theophilus, that God is the cause of all things, and, at the same time, that he can be no other than an inner cause. Now, if he is an inner cause of all things, how can you also call him a remote cause? Surely a cause cannot be both inner and remote.

THEOPHILUS: When I say that God is a remote cause, I only say it with reference to those things which God has produced indirectly, not with reference to those things which God has produced directly. But on no account did I mean that God is absolutely remote; it is only in this limited and specific respect that we call him remote.

ERASMUS: I now understand you more clearly. But you also say, with regard to an inner cause, that both cause and effect remain united, in such a way that together they constitute a whole. If this is so, it seems to me that God cannot be an inner cause. For if he, and that which is produced by him, together form a whole, then God would vary in dimension from one time to another. Please, clear up my confusion.

THEOPHILUS: If, Erasmus, you want to untangle yourself from your muddle, listen carefully to what I am going to tell you. The essence of a thing does not increase through its union with another thing with which it constitutes a whole. On the contrary, it remains unchanged. I shall give you an illustration, so that you can understand me better. A sculptor makes from a single lump of wood images of different parts of the human body. He takes the piece in the shape of a torso, and joins it to the piece in the shape of a head, so together they form the upper part of the body. You would not say that the essence of the head has been increased because it has been joined to the torso. On the contrary, you would say it was the same as before.

For greater clarity, let me give you another illustration. Take a triangle. Then stretch back two of the sides, until each is at right angles to the base. This has produced a new shape; yet it is connected with the triangle, in that the three angles of the triangle are equal to two right angles. In fact, the essence of the triangle remains unchanged.

The same is true for every idea which produces love. This love in no way adds to the essence of the idea.

But why multiply the illustrations? You can see clearly their purpose and meaning. I have said clearly that everything depends on God, and originates from God. Thus everything possesses the essence of God. And, as my illustrations have shown, God can cause a multiplicity of things without his essence increasing. He can therefore speak of Nature as a whole. If the different parts of Nature were unconnected, the whole would be no more than the sum of parts. But in fact the parts are connected because they share the same essence. Thus the whole is the unity of all parts.

ERASMUS: So far as this matter is concerned, you have satisfied me. But, in addition to this, you have also said that the effect of the inner cause cannot perish so long as its cause lasts. I can see this is true. Yet, since so many things perish, how can God be the inner cause of all things? In the light of what you have said already, I think I can anticipate your reply. You will say that those things produced directly by God cannot perish; but God is not the inner cause of those things produced indirectly by him, and therefore they can perish. But this does not satisfy me. You will declare that human understanding is immortal, since God himself produced it directly. This implies, it seems to me, that human understanding must have been created by God from all eternity, in common with all the other things produced directly by him.

Indeed, if I am not mistaken, I have heard you say this. But surely such a view leaves all sorts of difficulties unresolved.

THEOPHILUS: It is true, Erasmus, that the things produced directly by God have been created from all eternity ... But let us consider these things more carefully. Some are required in order to produce other things, while others are required so that other things are capable of being produced. For example, let us imagine I want light in a certain room. I kindle the light, and this lights up the room directly. Or I open a shutter; this act of opening does not itself give light, but it enables light to come into the room. Similarly, to set one body in motion, another body must already be in motion, and pass the motion on to it.

But for us to possess the idea of God, the process is rather different. The whole of Nature speaks of the presence of God. God is known only through himself; and in Nature we can know God directly. The challenge for human beings, therefore, is to have a clear idea of God in Nature, and hence be united with him in all our perceptions and actions. Then we shall realise that thought itself is produced directly by God. Without this sense of God in Nature, we cannot be united with him.

5
DEFINITION OF A PERSON

◆

from *God, Humans and their Well-Being*

Some regard the soul as having substance. In fact it is a mode or aspect of our existence. It consists of what we may broadly call thought.

Thought is an attribute of God. Thus is it not finite, but infinite, and therefore perfect.

Perfect thought must contain knowledge and ideas. This knowledge refers to that which is real, and has substance. Perfect thought embraces all knowledge: it knows the essence of all things, although it may not know each particular example of a thing.

This capacity for knowledge is what we call 'soul'. The capacity for motion and rest is what we call 'body'. The differences between bodies is determined by the different proportions of motion and rest. Some bodies have more motion, some have more rest. A particular soul contains special knowledge of its particular body.

A particular body has a particular proportion of motion and rest even as an unborn embryo. When it lives it has another proportion of motion and rest, and this will vary through life. And in death it will have yet another proportion. Yet, even while the body changes, there is a degree of constancy in the soul – in the way a person thinks and knows.

But the soul is not separate from the body. To some degree the proportion of motion and rest affects the soul, influencing the way the soul thinks and knows.

A person's identity lives in the soul, not the body, even though the body influences the soul. The soul is constantly subject to change, but only changes within narrow limits.

Apart from the soul's own body, the cause of change is the influence of other bodies and souls on it. The awareness of the change is what we call feeling.

The soul may be annihilated if the influences upon it are too violent. But it may become eternal if it unites with that which is eternal – if individual thought becomes united with divine thought, which is perfect.

6
THE DIVINE IDEA

from *God, Humans and their Well-Being*

In itself reason cannot fulfil us and make us happy. Therefore we must ask whether there is a particular kind of knowledge by which we could attain perfect happiness.

The kind of knowledge that leads to happiness does not come from a source that is distinct from happiness to the mind. And as the mind perceives happiness, it becomes united with it. To put it another way, the knowledge of happiness evokes love for happiness; in turn love for happiness evokes love for its sources, which we call God. God cannot reveal himself directly to us, but only through his blessing; in receiving his blessing we become united with him. In this union does our blessedness – our happiness – consist.

Thus I do not say that we must know God as he is, or even that we should know him adequately. It is sufficient to know him to some degree in order to be united with him. Even the knowledge we have of our own bodies is very particular: we do not know our bodies just as they are. Yet we are totally united with our bodies.

This knowledge of God is not the consequence of something else, but is immediate and direct. The knowledge of God is the cause of all other knowledge, and so must be acquired by itself alone. Moreover by our very nature we are united with God; so without him we can neither exist nor be known. This union with God is so close that it is evident we cannot know him except directly.

Let us then try to explain this union with God in more depth.

Everything that exists in Nature also exists as a divine idea. Indeed, we can speak of the Son of God as living the Idea that has existed from all eternity, and is made objective in Nature. And insofar as a thing approximates to perfection, that thing is in union with the divine Idea. Since this Idea is both infinite and unified, we can understand Nature in the same way: Nature is infinite in its variety and complexity, and yet has a single divine substance. The relationship of the individual soul to the body exemplifies the relationship of the divine Idea to Nature: the soul is aware of its own body, and is the cause of its life.

The relationship of the soul to the body, and of the divine Idea to Nature, is one of love. We can observe this union by observing ourselves. The feelings within the soul are consistently finding expression in the actions and movements of the body. Thus the union of the soul with the body is one of total sympathy. And when we become fully aware of this union, we may truly say that we have been born again. Our first birth took place when we were united with the body, and we became alive and active. The second birth takes place when we become aware of ourselves in our entirety, and love ourselves. In this way we become aware of the universe in its entirety: of material Nature, and of the divine Idea which animates it. And in this awareness we love Nature and the divine Idea. This second birth may justly be called 'regeneration', because our love unites us fully with that which is eternal and unchangeable – namely, God.

7
ANATOMY OF THE SOUL

from God, Humans and their Well-Being

Since humans are finite, created beings, it follows that human thought, and what we call the soul, is a mode or aspect of divine thought; and that the essence of a human being is this divine attribute. If thought were to cease, the soul would perish, even though divine thought continued. Similarly the human god is a mode or aspect of physical Nature. When the forces of Nature cease to flow through the body, then the body perishes – although Nature continues.

Let us try to understand more deeply this mode which we call soul, its relationship with the body, and how this relationship can change. We observe the following:

Firstly, thought contains the essence of all things. If you could suggest something that does not exist in Nature, then nor would it be contained in thought. Indeed, for this reason it is impossible to conceive of anything that does not in some sense exist in Nature. The explanation for this is that God is thought, and that God created Nature.

Secondly, all the other attributes of the soul, such

as love, desire, joy and so on, derive from thought; without thought there could be no love, desire and joy. The natural love which prompts the soul to preserve its body has its origin in the thought or idea of the body which the soul possesses ...

Lastly, it is impossible to speak of the soul as the object of thought, since this would imply that thought is located elsewhere from the soul. The soul can only be the object of thought in the sense that the soul can think about itself ...

Therefore the essence of the soul is the capacity for thought; and its relationship with Nature, including the body, is its ability to think about all things in Nature. Equally, the essence of all things in Nature is that they are the objects of thought, and owe this existence to divine thought. Yet you cannot properly speak of thought as the subject, and Nature as the object, since Nature arises from thought and is encompassed by thought. It is more correct to say that all things in Nature, and all human thought, are themselves attributes of God. Human thought is immediately and directly created by God, since God himself is thought. Thus all thought is unified in God ... Things in nature are indirectly created by God, since their immediate cause is something else in Nature ...

Returning to feelings, such as love, desire, joy and so on, we can see that these both derive from thought, and are the motives for thought. In particular feelings prompt the soul to reflect on itself, and on its relationship with other souls, with its body and other things in Nature, and with God. Feelings motivate the soul to unite its thought with the thought of God, because such unity gives rise to positive feelings. And once unity exists between God and the soul, then the soul is joined to the immortality of God, and can never perish.

8

THE NATURE OF GOD

from *Ethics*, Part 1

Apart from God nothing can exist or be conceived. Since God is absolutely infinite, and thus possesses all possible attributes, everything that does exist possesses particular attributes of God.

Whatsoever exists, exists in God; a thing can only exist or be conceived with God. God is that which exists in himself, and is conceived through himself. But all else exists only in the divine nature and through that alone can be conceived.

Many think of God as like a human being, consisting of a mind and body, and subject to emotions. Yet this notion is utterly alien to the truth. Anyone who thinks seriously about the divine nature must realise that God is not corporeal. A body has a certain height, width, size and shape. What could be more absurd than to say this about God?

God who is perfect in all things cannot be passive.

Everything is in God. All things which exist are made according to the nature of God, and manifest this nature. Thus God is infinitely active.

Since the divine nature has absolutely infinite

attributes, each of which expresses the divine nature, then there must be an infinity of creatures and an infinity of events.

All things fall under the infinite, divine intellect.

All things are determined and impelled by God's actions.

God is the immanent, not the transcendent, cause of all things. Since all things exist in God, all must be conceived in God. God is the cause of all things that are in him.

All the attributes of God are eternal.

The attributes of all things must exist for ever. The attributes, not the things themselves, are eternal.

When God determines that a thing must perform a certain function or purpose, that thing will perform that function and purpose.

In the universe nothing is contingent or accidental. All things are determined by God to exist and operate in a certain way.

All knowledge is ultimately knowledge of God.

Things could not have been produced by God in any other way or order than that in which they were produced. All things follow from the nature of God; and his nature determines their existence and actions. If things could have been determined in another way, so that the order of the universe were different, this would imply that God could have been different – and such a notion is absurd.

The power of God is his very essence.

People often ask: if all things have been created by the perfect wisdom of God, why are there so many faults in Nature? They point to the corruption and ugliness of many things, which nauseate and disgust the human senses; they point to confusion, evil and wrong-doing – and many other aspects of Nature which seem bad. The answer is that the perfection of things should be judged by their own standards, not by the degree to which they delight or disgust human beings, or whether human beings find them useful or harmful.

People often ask: why did God not create human beings in such a way that they are governed by reason alone. The reason is that, while all things are perfect, there are grades or levels of perfection. God's infinite intellect conceived all things of all grades; and having conceived them, he had of necessity to create them.

9

THE NATURE OF THE MIND

from *Ethics*, Part 2

Thought is an attribute of God, or, to put it another way, God is a thinking entity. Particular thoughts, about this or that express, in a certain and determinate way, the nature of God. So the attributes which all particular thoughts involve, and through which they are conceived, belong to God. It is one of his infinite attributes.

Most people believe that God possesses free will, and that he has total power. They say that he has the power to destroy everything, and to reduce it to nothing. And they often compare the power of God with that of things. But in truth God acts by necessity, through his own self-understanding; he acts according to the necessity of his own divine nature, performing infinite things in infinite ways. The power of God is nothing else than the essence of God.

The order and connection of ideas is the same as the order and connection of things. The idea that something has a cause depends on knowledge of that cause. It follow that God's power of thinking is equal to his actual power of acting.

The first thing which constitutes the functioning of a human mind is the idea of a particular thing actually existing.

The essence of a human being is the possession of God's attribute of thought.

The human mind is part of the infinite intellect of God. Thus when we say that the human mind perceives this or that, we are saying that God has this or that idea.

When we say that God has this or that idea, we are saying that the human mind perceives this or that in part.

Whatever happens in the human mind is known by God, in that he constitutes the nature of the human mind.

The primary object of the human mind is the body.

A human being consists of mind and body. The mind knows the body insofar as the mind senses the body.

The human mind perceives the nature of many bodies at the same time as it perceives the nature of its own body.

The mind has no knowledge of the body, nor is it even aware of the body's existence, except insofar as the senses are affected or disturbed.

The mind is normally confused in its knowledge of itself, its body and external bodies.

The mind has only a very inadequate knowledge of the duration of things.

Truth consists in knowledge being adequate, and tending towards perfection. Falsity consists in lack of knowledge or the corruption of knowledge.

People think they are free because they are conscious of their actions. But they are ignorant of the true causes by which these actions are determined.

People say that human actions depend on the will. But this statement has no meaning. No one knows what the will is, and where it is located in the human body.

Inadequate and confused ideas are as necessary for the human mind as adequate, clear and distinct ideas. All ideas are in God; and insofar as they have reference to God, they are true. But insofar as they have reference to a particular mind they are inadequate and confused.

Certain ideas and notions are common to all people. These ideas are adequate, clear and distinct.

The mind is more liable to perceive things adequately, the more it has in common with others.

A person who has a true idea knows it is true, and cannot doubt its truth. A true idea is that which is fully in God, and which God has made known to the human mind.

When we are certain of the truth of something, we know we are certain. Thus a true idea is itself a standard of truth. Just as light shows itself, and by contrast also shows darkness, so truth shows itself by its own standard, and by contrast shows falsity.

Every idea corresponding to something which actually exists involves the eternal and infinite essence of God.

The human mind has an adequate knowledge of the eternal and infinite essence of God.

People do not have as clear a knowledge of God as they do of particular things, because the infinity and eternity of God exceeds their imaginations.

The mind does not contain an absolute or free will. The ideas in the mind which lead to action are determined by a cause, which is determined by another cause, and so on infinitely backwards.

What appears to be human will is simply the expression of ideas.

Will and intellect are one and the same. They are an assembly of ideas.

10

THE NATURE OF EMOTIONS

from *Ethics*, Part 3

Those who have written about emotions mostly believe that human beings disturb, rather than follow, the laws of Nature, that they have absolute power over their own actions, and that they are psychologically independent. They then attribute human weakness and inconstancy not to the universal power of Nature, but to some defect or other in human nature.

Nothing happens in Nature which can be attributed to a defect in it. Nature is always the same, and its virtue and power of action is everywhere one and the same. The laws and rules of Nature, which determine how things are made and develop, are everywhere and always the same ... Therefore such emotions as hate, anger, envy and so on, considered in themselves, function according to Nature's laws, like everything else.

We can understand emotions by looking at their causes. We can know our emotions by contemplating their properties.

We can be called 'active' when the motive for action comes entirely from inside ourselves – from our emotions. We can be called 'passive' when the main spur to action comes from outside ourselves.

We are active insofar as our minds have adequate ideas. We are passive insofar as our minds have inadequate ideas.

When the mind has inadequate ideas, it is ruled by emotion. When the mind has adequate ideas, it is able to direct the emotions.

Decisions of the mind are prompted by emotions. Those who experience conflicting emotions cannot make decisions. Those who experience no emotions do not make decisions.

A decision, and the emotion prompting it, are really one and the same thing.

Anything may be the cause of pleasure, pain or desire.

When we have responded to something with the emotions of pleasure, we love that thing. When we have responded to something with the emotion of pain, we hate that thing.

Even if we only imagine something to be a cause of pleasure or pain, we love or hate that thing.

Emotions are affected not only by present experience, but by memories of the past and prospects for the future.

Hope is the pleasure which arises from a happy prospect. Fear is the pain which arises from an unhappy one. If doubt is removed from these emotions, hope becomes confidence, and fear becomes despair.

Joy is the pleasure arising from the memory of a happy event, whose occurrence had been in doubt. Disappointment is the pain from the memory of an unhappy event, whose occurrence had been in doubt.

When we think an object of love is affected by pleasure or pain, we feel pleasure or pain. The greater the love, the greater will be the congruence of emotions.

We cannot hate that which we pity, because its misery causes us pain.

We try to bring into existence everything which we imagine will be conducive to pleasure. We try to remove or destroy that which we think will be conducive to pain.

If we do something which affects those we love with pleasure, we feel pleasure.

If we think another person shares our emotions, our emotions are intensified.

When the love which we once had for an object turns to hatred, that hatred will be far stronger than if we had never loved.

If we think ourselves to be hated by another person, and believe we have given no cause for that hatred, we will hate in return.

The endeavour to inflict harm on those whom we

hate is called anger. The endeavour to inflict harm on those who have caused harm is called revenge.

Sometimes we both love and hate the same object. If hatred prevails over love, we may endeavour to inflict harm; and this is called cruelty.

Hatred is increased by reciprocal hatred, and can be destroyed by love.

Hatred which is entirely conquered by love becomes love; and such love is greater than if it had not been preceded by hatred.

Pleasure arises when we think that an object of hatred has been harmed or destroyed. But the pleasure is always offset by some pain.

The mind takes pleasure in its power of action.

The mind tries to think only of those things which connect with its power of action.

When the mind reflects on the limitations of its power of action, it feels pain.

The pain which arises when we reflect on our limitations and weakness is called humility. The pleasure which arises when we reflect on our power and strength of action is called pride.

People are naturally envious. This means they are prone to rejoice at the failure of others, and to be upset by their successes.

Envy makes people take pleasure in abilities which they themselves possess, and which others do not. But they take no pleasure in their own abilities, if these abilities are possessed by all human beings. Equally, envy makes people feel pained by the abilities which others possess, and which they themselves do not.

Our propensity toward hatred and envy is fostered in our upbringing. Parents often encourage their children to pursue success over their peers, judging their children by the degree to which they excel.

Envy only occurs between people who in general regard one another as equals.

There are as many types of pleasure, pain, love, hatred and so on, as there are objects of those emotions. But desire is common to them all, and predisposes the individual to action.

By gluttony, drunkenness, lust, avarice and ambition we understand the immoderate love of, and desire for, food, drinking, lechery, wealth and glory. These emotions are distinguished by having no opposites. Such attributes as temperance, sobriety, chastity and so on, which we usually contrast with those emotions, are not in themselves emotions. They indicate strength of mind, which moderates those emotions.

The emotions of animals differ from the emotions of human beings only inasmuch as their nature differs from ours.

All emotions are related to pleasure and pain, and hence to desire.

II

ANATOMY OF EMOTIONS

—————◆—————

from *Ethics*, Part 3

Desire is the essence of a human being, insofar as each human emotion can express itself as desire, and desire motivates human actions.

Joy is the passage from less to greater perfection.

Sorrow is the passage from greater to less perfection.

Astonishment is the imagination of an object, in which the mind remains fixed because this particular imagination has no connection with others.

Contempt is the imagination of an object which so little touches the mind that the mind is moved to reflect on those qualities which are not in the object, rather than those qualities which are in it.

Love is joy, when the mind is aware of the cause of joy.

Hatred is sorrow, when the mind is aware of the cause of sorrow.

Inclination is the idea that some object may be the cause of joy.

Aversion is the idea that some object may be the cause of sorrow.

Devotion is love towards an object which astonishes us.

Derision is the idea that something we despise is contained in an object we hate.

Hope is a joy which is not constant, arising from the idea of something in the future, of whose consequences we are uncertain.

Fear is a sorrow which is not constant, arising from the idea of something in the future, of whose consequences we are uncertain.

Confidence is joy arising from the idea of something in the future, whose cause for doubting has been removed.

Despair is sorrow arising from the idea of something in the future, whose cause for doubting has been removed.

Gladness is joy arising from the recollection of something past which, unhoped for, has occurred.

Remorse is sorrow arising from the recollection of something past which, though not feared, has occurred.

Commiseration is sorrow, arising from the idea of something evil which has happened to someone like ourselves.

Favour is love towards those who have benefited others.

Indignation is hatred towards those who have injured others.

Over-estimation consists in thinking too highly of another person as a result of love for that person.

Contempt consists in thinking too little of another person as a result of hatred for that person.

Envy is hatred, expressing itself as sadness at the good fortune of another person, and gladness at an evil that happens to that person.

Compassion is love, expressing itself as gladness at the good fortune of another person, and sadness at any evil that happens to that person.

Self-satisfaction is the joy produced by contemplating our own power of action.

Humility is the sorrow produced by contemplating our own impotence and helplessness.

Repentance is sorrow accompanied by the idea of something we have done, which we believed we did freely.

Pride is thinking too much of ourselves, through self-love.

Despondency is thinking too little of ourselves, through self-hatred.

Self-exaltation is joy, with the idea of some action we have done which we imagine others praise.

Shame is sorrow, with the idea of some action we have done which we imagine others blame.

Regret is the desire or longing to possess something, accompanied by the memory of that object, and the memory of other things which prevent the possession of that object.

Emulation is a desire within us, which has been kindled by the belief that other people have the same desire.

Gratitude is the desire, arising from love, to do good to others, who, also from love, have done good to us.

Benevolence is the desire to do good to those whom we pity.

Anger is the desire by which we are impelled, through hatred, to injure those whom we hate.

Vengeance is the desire, springing from mutual hatred, to injure those who have injured us.

Cruelty is the desire which impels people to injure those whom they love or pity.

Fear is the desire to avoid evil.

Audacity is the desire to do something which is dangerous, and of which others are frightened.

Consternation occurs when our desire to avoid some evil is restrained by our astonishment that the evil exists.

Courtesy is the desire to do things which please others, and to avoid doing things which displease them.

Ambition is the immoderate desire for glory.

Greed is the immoderate desire for comfort.

Avarice is the immoderate desire for riches.

Lust is the immoderate desire for sex.

12
GOOD AND EVIL

———◆———

from *Ethics*, Part 3

Let me say a few words about perfection and imperfection, and about good and evil. If you have prepared to do something, and have accomplished it, you call it perfect; and not only you, but all who have known your purpose and intention, will call it perfect too. For example, if we see a building which is half completed, and which we know is intended to be a house, we call it imperfect. But as soon as the house is completed, just as the builder intended, we call it perfect. On the other hand, if we see some work which we have not seen before, and we do not know the intention of the person doing it, we shall not know whether to call the work perfect or imperfect. This, at any rate, is the primary meaning of the words 'perfect' and 'imperfect'.

Yet humans also possess universal ideas. They have thought out for themselves different ways of erecting houses, churches and castles, preferring one way to another. So we call a particular thing perfect because it conforms to the universal idea we have of that thing; and we call something imperfect insofar as it fails to conform to that universal idea – even though it may have fulfilled the intentions of the person who made it. This appears to be the only reason why the words 'perfect' and 'imperfect' are commonly applied to objects not made by human hands. We have the habit of forming universal ideas about natural as well as artificial objects, based on our conception of Nature's intentions – in the belief that Nature does nothing except for some purpose.

Conversely, when we see a natural object that does not conform to our universal idea, we are apt to say that Nature has committed an error, and that the object is imperfect. Thus we can see that the custom of applying the words 'perfect' and 'imperfect' to natural objects has arisen more from prejudice than from true knowledge.

In fact Nature does nothing for a purpose. Nature is embraced within that eternal and infinite being whom we call God; and God acts by the necessity of his own nature. Thus the actions of Nature and the nature of God are one and the same. God exists for no purpose and he acts for no purpose. The only sense in which we can speak of 'purpose' or 'cause' is in relation to human desire. For example, when someone builds a house to live in, we may say that the desire for a dwelling is the cause of that house being built. Yet we are merely saying that a person imagined the advantages of domestic life, and so built a house ... But desire is not the ultimate or final cause of such an action; it is the immediate motivation.

Thus perfection and imperfection are really only modes of thought. They are notions which we are in the habit of forming, by comparing one example of a species or genus with another. Yet in truth 'perfection' is another word for reality. Ultimately all objects are examples or expressions of the one universal idea, embracing Nature as a whole. When we call something imperfect, we are merely saying that it does not affect our minds so strongly as something which we call perfect. But this reflects our way of thinking, not the object itself. Everything in Nature belongs to Nature; and hence everything in Nature belongs to God, and follows from the necessity of God.

With regard to good and evil, these terms indicate nothing positive in things considered in themselves, nor are they anything else but modes of thought – notions we form by comparing one thing with another. One and the same thing may simultaneously be good, evil or indifferent. A particular piece of music may comfort one person who is sad, depress another person who is worried, and have no impact on a third person who is deaf. Nonetheless we need to retain the words 'good' and 'evil'. This is because we need to form for ourselves a model of human nature to which we can aspire. And then we should use the word 'good' for the ways in which we conform to that model; and the word evil for everything that hinders us from conforming to it.

Thus when I say that a man passes from lesser to greater perfection, or vice versa, I do not mean that he has changed from one essence to another. Rather I mean that he has fulfilled his own nature; he has become more fully himself, conforming more closely to the model to which, consciously or unconsciously, he aspires.

Finally, let me return to my assertion that 'perfection' and 'reality' are the same. For an object to be perfect, it has to exist and act according to its nature; it has to fulfil its reality. This is not connected to duration. An object is not more perfect because it has fulfilled itself for a longer period. What matters is that it exists for as long as its nature requires it to exist.

Thus we can conclude that in truth all things and all people are equal.

THE STRENGTH OF EMOTIONS

from *Ethics*, Part 4

By servitude I mean the lack of power to moderate and check the emotions. Those who submit to their emotions do not have power over themselves, but are in the hands of fortune. They may see what is better for themselves, but are forced to follow what is worse.

The words good and bad should be used to refer to the degree to which human nature attains perfection. To be good is to grow towards a state of perfection; to be bad is to fall away from that state.

To become perfect does not mean changing one's nature; it means that one's existing nature is not perfect.

At particular times different emotions may pull us in different directions. This is not caused by the nature of the emotions themselves, but by particular circumstances.

Virtue is the power to act according to one's perfect nature.

By their nature human beings are subject to emotions. What matters is this relationship with their emotions.

The force of an emotion can overwhelm our power of action.

An emotion can only be impeded or suppressed by a contrary emotion which is stronger.

True knowledge of good and bad cannot in itself restrain an emotion. It can only do so if it is itself attached to an emotion.

Desire which arises from a true knowledge of good and bad can be destroyed or checked by many other desires.

Desire which arises from pleasure is necessarily stronger than desire which arises from pain.

Some emotions agree with the rules of human reason, and some do not.

The basis of virtue is the endeavour to preserve one's own being; and happiness consists in virtue.

Virtue should be desired for its own sake. There is nothing more excellent and more useful to us than the desire for virtue.

Those who are governed by reason, and under its guidance seek what is most useful to them, desire nothing for themselves which they do not desire for the rest of humanity. Therefore they are just, faithful and honourable.

The knowledge of good is linked to an emotion of pleasure. The knowledge of bad is linked to an emotion of pain. For this reason human beings naturally seek what is good, and reject what is bad.

The more we try to act virtuously, the more virtuous we become. The less we try to act virtuously, the less power we have over our emotions. Virtue is the essence of power.

Virtue has no meaning apart from the nature of the person acting virtuously.

Human beings, insofar as their ideas are inadequate, cannot act virtuously. They act virtuously only to the extent that they have knowledge and insight.

To act virtuously is to act under the guidance of reason.

Actions are good if they help us to understand our nature, and to perfect our nature. Actions are bad if they hinder our understanding.

To understand and perfect our nature means to understand the perfection of God.

Insofar as people are slaves to their emotions, they are not living according to their natures.

People differ in the extent to which they are slaves to their emotions, and in the emotions which have the greatest power over them.

Insofar as people live under the guidance of reason, they are living according to their natures.

The most valuable thing a person can do is to get to know another person who lives under the guidance of reason.

The greatest good of those who follow the path of virtue is to know God. This is a good which can be possessed equally by all people, and which is potentially common to all.

Those who follow the path of virtue desire the same good for others as they desire for themselves.

Do not trust particular emotions or desires unless you understand how they relate to life as a whole.

Some people are so frightened of doing wrong that they do not do good either.

Reason enables us to distinguish between competing goods. We can follow the greater of two goods, and the lesser of two evils.

To be free means to have adequate knowledge, and to live according to that knowledge.

If people were born free, and had adequate knowledge from the beginning, they would form no conception of bad. Thus they would also form no conception of good.

The free person is equally good at avoiding dangers as at overcoming them.

A free person has the same courage to fight as presence of mind to take flight.

Only free people are truly grateful to one another. This is because freedom is necessary to forge true bonds of friendship, in which individuals love and serve one another.

The gratitude of people with inadequate knowledge who are led by undirected desire, is not true gratitude, because their relationships with others are based on mutual advantage rather then true love.

People can enjoy greater freedom in a society guided by common decision than they can in solitude.

14
THE POWER OF THE MIND

———◆———

from *Ethics*, Part 5

We are able to detach an emotion from its external stimulus, and unite it in the mind to other thoughts. This dissolves the love or hatred which existed towards the external cause.

We can only direct and channel our emotions insofar as we understand them clearly and distinctly.

Once we realise that all objects and events are in God, and God is in them, we are better able to control our emotions towards them.

No emotion is contrary to our nature if we make the right connections in our minds.

Insofar as we do not have adequate knowledge of our emotions, we are wise to adopt rules for living, based on the experience of others, committing those rules to memory and applying them in the various situations we encounter.

The most important rule for living is that hatred should not be reciprocated by hatred, but by love and generosity.

Those who understand themselves and their emotions clearly, love God. And those who truly and sincerely love God, understand themselves and their emotions clearly.

Love of God draws all the emotions together into unity.

No one who knows God can hate God.

Those who love God do not try to make God love them in return. If they desired this, their emotion would not be love.

The more we understand particular things, the more we understand God.

Although prompted by the emotions, love of God exists in the mind. Mental love of God is the same love by which God loves himself.

Since God loves himself, and since God created human beings with the same facility for love, God loves human beings.

Although the individual mind is not eternal, it is part of that which is eternal.

Blessedness is not the reward for virtue; it is virtue.

The capacity to direct our emotions does bring virtue. On the contrary, virtue expresses itself in the capacity to direct our emotions.

Ignorant people are guided by emotions of desire alone; wise people direct and harmonise desires. Ignorant people are unaware of themselves, God, and the divine nature of the objects around them. Wise people are aware of themselves, God, and the divine nature of the objects around them. Ignorant people are never content; wise people are always content.

Although the road I have shown is hard, everyone is capable of treading it. Indeed it must be hard, because it is so rarely trodden. If salvation were close at hand and easy to discover, more people would find it. But all excellent things are as difficult as they are rare.

15
MISCELLANEOUS REFLECTIONS

---

from Spinoza's Letters, 1665–76

To me the greatest blessing is to enter into the bonds of friendship with those who sincerely love the truth. We can enjoy great peace through loving such people. And it is impossible to break these bonds of love, because they are forged by the love each one has for the truth.

The truth is beyond our power to change or manipulate. Thus the truth can unite people with different prejudices and temperaments.

It follows from God's providence, which is the same as his will, and also from God's perpetual creation of things, either that there are no sins and no evil, or that God causes sins and evil.

Many people think of evil and sin as being deliberately opposed to the will of God ... But I cannot regard sin and evil as something positive in that sense. Nothing can exist or occur against the will of God. Far from regarding sin as something positive, I believe that it betrays the limitations of human understanding to say that we sin against God and that we make God angry.

Everything, considered in itself and without regard to anything else, includes perfection.

We see in Nature wars between bees, jealousy between doves – all sorts of things which in humans we would detest, but in other creatures we regard as part of their nature, and hence as a manifestation of their perfection.

It would surely suggest that God were profoundly imperfect if things were to happen against his will, and if he were to desire something which he could not obtain. And it would also be opposed to his nature if he were to have sympathy towards some of his creatures, and antipathy towards others.

Evil is no more than the privation of the perfect state.

We can only speak of the privation of the perfect state in relation to our own understanding, not in relation to God.

The more perfection a person has, the more they participate in God, and the more perfectly they express his perfection.

Those who have no knowledge of God are no more than tools in the hand of the craftsman, serving the craftsman unconsciously. Those who know God serve him consciously, and so become more perfect in his service.

I say that God is absolutely and effectively the cause of everything that is positive, and real in itself.

If I can be shown that some evil or villainy is something positive and real, I shall fully accept that God is the cause. But I am convinced that evil and villainy are not positive and real, and hence do not love God as their cause ... People do deeds, which we call evil, because they lack gratitude, lack mercy, lack compassion and so on. Evil is not positive and real, but is negative; it stems from the lack of some attribute of perfection. Thus God is not the cause.

We should distinguish between philosophy and theology. Usually theology represents God as a perfect human being; so it is quite appropriate for theology to speak of God as desiring something, as being weary of the deeds of the ungodly, and as taking pleasure in the deeds of the pious. But in philosophy we understand that to apply to God the attributes of human beings is as foolish as applying to human beings the attributes of an elephant or a donkey. In other words, theology confuses terms, and so confuses our minds. So speaking philosophically we cannot say that God demands something from someone, or that something wearies him or pleases him, because these are human attributes, which have no place in God.

The difference between the godly and the ungodly is that the godly have a clear idea of God, and their thoughts and actions are determined by that idea; whereas the ungodly do not have a clear idea of

God, and are therefore also confused about earthly things – which means their thoughts and actions are confused and contradictory.

People often judge an action by whether it is good in relation to God. They say that the righteous person does some good to God, and the thief some evil. In fact neither the righteous person nor the thief can cause either pleasure or pain to God ... But if you ask whether the thief and the righteous person are equally blessed, the answer is, 'No'. The righteous person firmly desires to love in harmony with God, and thus seeks a clear knowledge of God. The thief has no such desire.

To know one part of Nature is to know the whole; to know the whole of Nature is to know one part.

The human mind cannot perceive the whole of Nature; the mind is finite, whereas Nature is infinite. But the mind can perceive one part of Nature; and for this reason I say that the individual mind is one part of the infinite mind of God.

We cannot understand God, but we can conceive God. We cannot know him in his entirety, but we can understand some of his attributes.

FURTHER READING

Ethics is available in both Everyman or Penguin classics editions. An excellent *Selection* was compiled by John Wild and published by Charles Scribner's Sons in 1930. It includes the whole of *Ethics*, and the two earlier treatises, *On the Improvement of the Understanding*, and *God, Humans and their Well-Being*; it also has a number of his letters.

PHILOSOPHERS OF THE SPIRIT

Chuang Tzu

- What is the true Way, that leads to balance and harmony?
- Can people dichotomy the opposite of action and inaction, success and failure, joy and sorrow?
- Can rulers and subjects all be free?

The Chinese philosopher Chuang Tzu, who died around 310 BC, is one of the great founders of Taoism. His teaching is both comic and profound, filled with startling paradoxes and enigmatic stories. And from it emerges a practical philosophy which promises its adherents particular serenity.

PHILOSOPHERS OF THE SPIRIT

Also in this series

Eckhart

- Can God be born in all people?
- Is it possible to be continually serene and tranquil?
- Should the free spirit refuse to pray?

Condemned as a heretic, Eckhart taught that the spiritual path is not a matter of belief, but of inner experience. He shows his followers how God can be born in the individual soul, so that each person may become like Christ.

PHILOSOPHERS OF THE SPIRIT

Also in this series

Hildegard

- Are the spiritual and material realms separate, or are they two aspects of a whole?
- Can human beings change to live in greater harmony with one another and with their environment

A twelfth-century German mystic and philosopher, Hildegard is being rediscovered as a musical composer and as a prophet of the environmental movement. In her visions, she saw God in all living things. She saw that human beings can find inner peace only if they recognise their spiritual unity with animals and plants. Her insights into the human psyche seem astonishingly modern.

PHILOSOPHERS OF THE SPIRIT

Also in this series

Kierkegaard

- Is truth objective?
- Can we make real moral choices, or are our choices pre-determined?
- Who are the true saints and heroes of this world?

Kierkegaard, the nineteenth-century Danish philosopher, is both one of the most difficult and one of the most attractive thinkers of the modern period. He is regarded as the founder of existentialism.

This selection of his works, together with an easily readable summary of the principles of his thought and an outline of his life, offers a straightforward introduction to his complex ideas.

PHILOSOPHERS OF THE SPIRIT

Also in this series

Pascal

- Are science and mathematics the only means of searching for truth?
- Is religious faith a gamble?
- Why are human beings obsessed with goals that cannot be realized?

Blaise Pascal, writing in the seventeenth century, was both scientist and philosopher. He found a way of combining rational and religious scepticism. In penetrating and often witty epigrams, he saw clearly the paradoxes and dilemmas of the human condition, and he concluded that gambling on faith was the only way of resolving them.

PHILOSOPHERS OF THE SPIRIT

Also in this series

Rumi

- Is truth found in the resolution of opposites?
- Does knowledge come from making the heart rule the head?
- Is freedom a manifestation of destiny?

Rumi is recognised as the leading Sufi philosopher. Living in the thirteenth century CE, he was the founder of the Mevlevi Order of Sufis – the so-called Whirling Dervishes – who sought to obtain spiritual knowledge through dance and other forms of passionate worship. While rooted in Islam, Rumi incurred the wrath of the more legalistic Islam leaders. But his ideas and practices spread rapidly throughout the Middle East; and he still has thousands of followers.

PHILOSOPHERS OF THE SPIRIT

Also in this series

Socrates

- Is preparation for death the real purpose of life?
- Can we enjoy true happiness only apart from the body?

Socrates, the great teacher of ancient Athens, was a philosopher and a mystic – and a notorious debunker. He wrote nothing down, and our only reliable witness is the works of his disciple Plato. Condemned to death by his enemies, the account of his final hours is one of the highlights of classical literature.